RANGERS
CHANGING FACES

Rangers 1876–77. Back row, left to right: George Gillespie, William McNeil, James Watt, Sam Ricketts. Middle row: William Dunlop, David Hill, Tom Vallance, Peter Campbell, Moses McNeil. Front row: James Watson, Alex Marshall.

RANGERS
CHANGING FACES

ANDREW L. STEVENSON

FONTHILL

Acknowledgements

Many of the photos contained in this volume come from my own private collection. However, many sources have been of great assistance in compiling this pictorial history of Rangers FC and to this end I extend my thanks to the following people and newspapers:

Joe Ellis, Paul Lunney, Stuart Marshall, Jack Murray, the *Glasgow Herald, Daily Record, Scottish Daily Express*, DC Thomson and of course, Rangers FC.

Fonthill Media Limited
www.fonthillmedia.com
office@fonthillmedia.com

First published in the United Kingdom 2014

British Library Cataloguing in Publication Data:
A catalogue record for this book is available from
the British Library

ISBN 978-1-78155-083-0

Typeset in 9.5pt on 12pt Mrs Eaves Serif Narrow.
Printed and bound in England

Introduction

Rangers FC were formed in 1872, but if any photographs of their early teams were taken then they have long been lost to Father Time.

The earliest known image of a Rangers eleven in existence is that of the side which reached the Scottish Cup Final in 1877, and rather appropriately, is the first picture in this collection.

Rangers Changing Faces is my attempt to produce as many team photos, from the Victorian era to the present day, as possible. These, together with various player profiles, give the viewer some idea of how the kit and facial expressions of the players have changed over the passing decades.

Here, for the first time, 102 First Team group photos are on display, and never before has the identity of so many Rangers players been revealed.

I hope you enjoy viewing this pictorial history of Rangers teams and stars of the past every bit as much as I did in putting this volume together.

Andrew L. Stevenson

'Honest Tom' Vallance was a founder member of Rangers in 1872 and club captain for nine seasons from its inception. A noted athlete, his long jump record of 21 feet 11 inches at Queen's Park Sports in 1881 stood for fourteen years. President of Rangers from 1883-1889, Tom Vallance was also a gifted artist, exhibiting at the Royal Glasgow Institute and the Scottish Academy. A talented rower and keen golfer he was capped seven times by Scotland at football. Born in Succoth, near Renton, Dumbartonshire in 1856, Tom Vallance died at 189 Pitt Street in Glasgow's city centre on 16 February 1935, aged seventy-eight.

The Rangers players and their opponents (a Canadian XI) line up to have their photo taken on 8 September 1888. The match ended in a 1-1 draw.

The Rangers team of 1890-91 which were declared joint champions with Dumbarton after a decider ended in a 2-2 draw.

Dundee and Rangers players line-up for this historical photograph, which was taken to celebrate Dundee's first Scottish League match on 12 August 1893. The game ended in a 3-3 draw.

The first Rangers team to win the Scottish Cup in 1894. Back row, left to right: H. McCreadie, J. Steel, N. Smith, J. Taylor (trainer), D. Haddow, D. Mitchell. Middle row: A. McCreadie, D. Boyd, W. Wilton (secretary), J. Drummond, J. McPherson, J. Barker. Front row: R. Marshall, J. Gray.

Rangers 1896-97. Back row, left to right: T. Low, M. Dickie, N. Smith, J. Miller, J. Muir (committee), T. Hyslop, A. Smith, J. Oswald, R. G. Neil. Front row: J. McPherson, N. Gibson, D. Mitchell, A. McCreadie, T. Turnbull. Inset J. Drummond.

Rangers 1897.

League Champions 1898-99. Back row, left to right: N. Smith, D. Crawford, N. Gibson, M. Dickie, J. Stark, R. G. Neil, J. T. Robertson, J. Drummond. Front row, left to right: J. Campbell, J. Graham, J. McPherson, R. C. Hamilton, F. Speedie, A. Sharp, A. Smith. Insets: J. Miller, D. Mitchell, J. Wilkie, T. Hyslop.

Above left: John 'Kitey' McPherson. A Scottish Internationalist and Rangers forward of the 1890s.

Above right: Matt Dickie, Rangers brilliant goalkeeper from 1895 to 1904. Capped 3 times by Scotland.

A faded photo of Rangers invincible League side of 1898-99.

Rangers 1898-99. Back row, left to right: N. Smith, J. Miller, D. Crawford, J. Wilkie, M. Dickie, J. Taylor (trainer). Front row: J. Campbell, J. McPherson, A. Sharp, R. C. Hamilton, A. Smith, N. Gibson, R. G. Neil, D. Mitchell.

Scottish Internationalist Neil Gibson, Rangers great wing-half from 1894 to 1904 when he signed for Partick Thistle. Father of three footballing sons of the 1920s – Jimmy, Willie and Neil Junior.

Above left: Left-back David Crawford joined Rangers from St Mirren in 1894 and returned to the Paisley outfit in 1903.

Above right: Winger John Campbell signed for the 'Light Blues' from Blackburn Rovers in 1898 and moved onto West Ham United in 1902.

Above left: Highlander Bob Hamilton's career began at Elgin City and Rangers signed him from Queen's Park in 1897. A prolific goalscorer he was a schoolmaster by profession.

Above right: Known as the 'Prince of Centre-Forwards' and 'Toffee Bob', R. S. McColl had a distinguished career with Queen's Park, Newcastle United, Rangers and Scotland from 1894 to 1910.

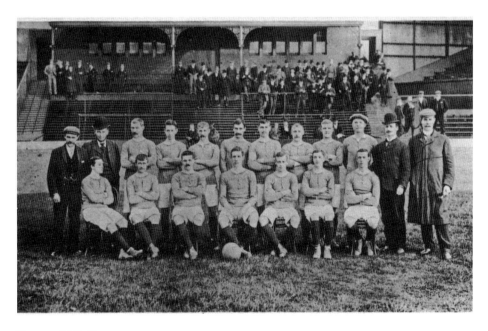

Rangers 1900-01.

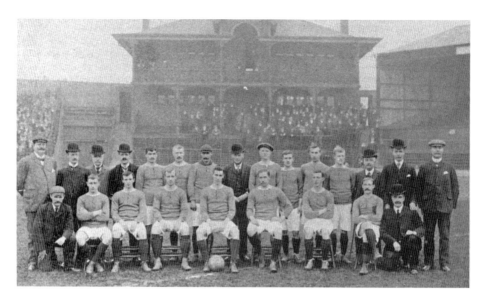

Rangers 1902-03.

Above left: A full back with Celtic, R. G. Campbell cost Rangers £350 in January 1906 and played in a number of outfield positions for the 'Light Blues' including centre forward and centre half. Subsequently a director of the club, Bob was an assiduous worker for the Glasgow Wesleyan Brotherhood. He collapsed and died in Bath Street on 31 May 1943, aged sixty.

Above right: Rugged half-back Jacky Robertson starred for Morton, Everton and Southampton before joining Rangers fro £300 in 1899. He became Chelsea's first manager in 1905 and subsequently coached on the continent.

Born in Galway on 2 April 1886, Irishman Alec Craig joined Rangers from Rutherglen Glencairn in March 1905. An excellent full-back he represented Northern Ireland on nine occasions and subsequently starred in defence for Morton.

Solid and reliable centre-half Jimmy Stark arrived at Ibrox from Glasgow Perthshire in May 1900. Capped twice by Scotland, Stark also represented the Scottish League on a couple of occasions, and went on to play for Chelsea and Morton.

Skilful forward Alec Bennett is undoubtedly the most decorated footballer to play at both Rangers and Celtic. He made eleven appearances for Scotland and a further ten for the Scottish League. Bennett signed for the 'Light Blues' as a 'free agent' in May 1908 and subsequently starred at Dumbarton and Albion Rovers.

Rangers 1908-09. Back row, left to right: Noble, Jackson, Bennett, Gordon. Middle row: Rennie, Galt, Taylor, MacDonald, Law, Murray. Front row: Craig, MacPherson, Gilchrist, Campbell, Sharp, Livingstone, Smith.

Rangers 1909-10. Back row, left to right: W. Yuille, J. McLean, J. Stark, R. G. Campbell, J. Galt, J. Gordon, J. May, W. Hunter. Middle row: H. Rennie, G. Waddell, W. Reid, T. Gilchrist, G. Law, A. Thomson, W. McPherson, H. Lock. Front row: J. Wilson (trainer), A. Bennett, T. Miller, W. Hogg, J. McKenzie, A. Craig, J. Jackson, A. Smith.

Rangers 1910-11. Back row, left to right: W. Hogg, D. Taylor, G. Chapman, H. Lock, J. Galt, R. G. Campbell, J. Hendry, A. Cunningham, A. Gibson, J. Wilson (trainer). Front row: A. Bennett, W. Reid, W. Yuill, G. B. Waddell, J. Gordon, R. Parker, G. Law, A. Smith. Insets: R. Brown, A. Richmond.

Rangers 1911-1912. Back row, left to right: J. Wilson (trainer), Ormond, Chapman, Campbell, Galt, Hogg, Cameron, Reid, Richmond, Gibson, Law. Middle row: Boden, Gordon, Waddell, Bowie, Lock, Bennett, parker, Smith. Front row: R. Brown, Paterson, Goodwin, A. Brown, Hendry.

'Rangers Great' Willie Reid specialised in first-time swerving shots which gave goalkeepers no chance of saving. He played for Morton, Third Lanark, Motherwell and Portsmouth before arriving at Ibrox in 1909. Capped nine times by Scotland, Reid was manager of Albion Rovers in the 1920s and Dundee United in the 1930s.

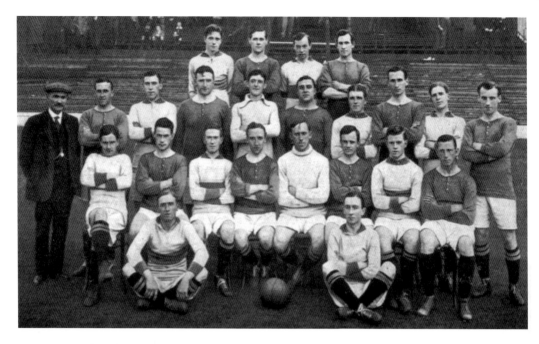

Rangers 1912-13. Back row, left to right: Riddell, Hendry, Paterson, Robertson. Middle row: J. Wilson (trainer), Montgomery, Ormond, Campbell, Hogg, Ferguson, Galt, Lawrie, Gordon. Front row: Boden, Reid, R. Brown, Bowie, Lock, Bennett, Parker, Smith. Ground: A. Brown and Goodwin.

Rangers 1914-15. Back row, left to right: H. Lock, J. Hempsey, J. Muir. Middle row: W. Struth, J. Hendry, P. Pursell, T. Kelso, R. Brown, J. Logan, H. Muir, A. Craig, G. Dickson, J. Paterson, T. Gilchrist. Front row: W. Reid, A. S. Duncan, J. Bowie, T. Cairns, A. Bennett, J. Gordon, A. Smith.

Outside right Billy Hogg.

Outside left Jimmy Paterson.

Centre half James L. Logan.

Full back George Ormond.

Sturdy and direct outside right Sandy Archibald was a key member and a mainstay of Rangers successful sides between the wars. Capped eight times by Scotland, he went on to manage Fife clubs Raith Rovers and Dunfermline Athletic before his early death in November 1946, aged forty-nine.

Industrious inside left Tommy Cairns joined Rangers from St Johnstone in 1913 and gave the Ibrox club excellent service until transferring to Bradford City in 1927. Cairns made eight Scotland and six Scottish League appearances. Arsenal's Scottish scout in the 1930s, he died in December 1967, aged seventy-seven.

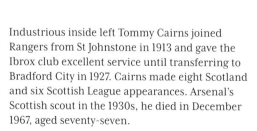

Rangers 1919-20. Back row, left to right: McQueen, Lawson, Walls, Manderson. Middle row: W. Struth (trainer), Cunningham, Davidson, Gordon, Lock, Cairns, Henderson. Front row: Archibald, Muirhead, Bowie, Reid, Dixon.

Tall inside forward Andy Cunningham could play anywhere on the football field and was a specialist at the defence-splitting through-pass. After fourteen years with Rangers, he joined Newcastle United in 1929 and became their first manager the following year. One of Scottish football's all-time greats, he represented Scotland and the Scottish League on many occasions.

Rangers 1920-21. Back row, left to right: Cunningham, Smith, McQueen, Meiklejohn, Lawson, Sutherland, McDonald, McMillan, Cairns. Middle row: Livingstone (trainer), Walls, Reid, Lock, Manderson, Robb, McKenna, Archibald. Front row: Laird, Dixon, Henderson, Bowie, Low, Muirhead, Johnston, Morton.

Rangers 1922-23. Back row, left to right: MacDonald, Reid, Kirkwood, Walls, Kilpatrick, Ireland, Rollo, Roberts, McCandless. Middle row: W. Struth (manager), Hamilton, Meiklejohn, Jamieson, Craig, Nicholson, Henderson, Johnston, Dixon, Lawson, Robb, Livingstone (trainer). Front row: Archibald, Muirhead, Cairns, Manderson, Cunningham, Morton, Hansen.

Rangers 1926-27. Back row, left to right: Purdon, Hodge, Smith, Ashborne, Moyes, Hamilton, McGregor, Manderson, Fleming, McKay. Middle row: Chalmers, Archibald, Craig, Ireland, Kirkwood, Shaw, Henderson, Cunningham, Weir. Front row: W. Struth (manager), Meiklejohn, Gray, Morton, Dixon, Cairns, Muirhead, Marshall, Livingstone (trainer).

Rangers 1927-28. Back row, left to right: McPhail, Hair, Shaw, Moyes, Cunningham, R. Hamilton. Middle row: Meiklejohn, Lockie, Marshall, Ireland, Craig, Docherty, Archibald, J. Hamilton, Fleming, Simpson, Gray, Osborne, T. Hamilton. Front row: McCandless, McMillan, Muir head, Chalmers, Morton.

Rangers Scottish Cup Winners 1928. Back row, left to right: 'Tully' Craig, Davie Meiklejohn, Andy Cunningham, Sandy Archibald, Bob Hamilton, Jimmy Bowie (director), Tom Hamilton, Jimmy Fleming, James Kerr (trainer), James Marshall, Jack Buchanan. Front row: Dougie Gray, Joseph Buchanan (chairman), Bill Struth (manager), Tommy Muirhead, Alan Morton, Bob McPhail.

Rangers in Chicago on their summer tour of the USA and Canada in 1928.

A 'Wembley Wizard' of 1928, Alan Morton joined Rangers from Queen's Park in June 1920. A tricky winger with intricate skills, as Bill Struth's first signing 'Pinky' proved to be a key component of the Rangers sides which dominated the Scottish football scene of the 1920s. He retired in 1933 to become a club director and remained one until June 1971. 'The Wee Blue Devil' died on 15 December 1971.

Rangers 1928-29. Back row, left to right: Directors – D. Graham, J. Buchanan, J. Bowie, W. R. Simpson. Middle row: Archibald, Fleming, Meiklejohn, T. Hamilton, Cunningham, R. Hamilton, Buchanan. Front row: W. Struth (manager), Gray, Craig, Muirhead, McPhail, Moron, J. Kerr (trainer).

Rangers 1929-30. Back row, left to right: Jimmy Fleming, James Marshall, Alan Morton, Tom Hamilton, Billy McCandless, Jock Buchanan. Front row: Bob McPhail, Sandy Archibald, Dougie Gray, Davie Meiklejohn, Tommy Muirhead, Tully Craig.

The Rangers players at St Enock Station on their return from a summer tour of Canada in 1930.

Rangers 1930-31. Back row, left to right: Dawson, Marshall, Purdon, Buchanan, Smith, McDonald, Conlin, R. Hamilton, T. Hamilton. Middle row: Main, Archibald, Lockie, McPhail, Simpson, Fleming, Murray, Meiklejohn, W. Struth (manager). Front row: J. Kerr (trainer), Nicholson, Brown, Gray, McMillan, Muirhead, Osborne, Craig, Morton.

Rangers 1930-31. Back row, left to right: J. Kerr (trainer), Meiklejohn, Marshall, Archibald, Fleming, T. Hamilton, Buchanan, Craig. Front row: Brown, Gray, McDonald, Muirhead, McPhail, R. Hamilton, Nicholson, Morton.

Rangers 1931-32.

Leading left half of the 1930s, George Brown joined Rangers from Ashfield in 1929. On retirement from playing in 1942, he became a director – a position he held until 1979, thus giving fifty years service to the club. Capped nineteen times by Scotland, George Brown died in June 1988, aged eighty-one.

Bob McPhail accepts a gift of flowers before Rangers friendly match against a Germany Select in 1933.

Alan Morton congratulates Celtic centre forward Jimmy McGrory on his Benefit match at Parkhead on 27 August 1934. Result: Celtic 0 Rangers 4.

Rangers 1934-35. Back row, left to right: Dawson, Gillick, Craig, hmilton, McDonald, Fleming, Jenkins. Middle row: W. Struth (manager), Marshall, Cheyne, Simpson, Kennedy, Smith, Drysdale, McPhail, Dixon (trainer). Front row: Main, McAuley, Gray, Venters, Meiklejohn, Hart, Brown, Archibald, Nicholson.

Rangers 1935-36. Back row, left to right: Dawson, Cheyne, Hart, Brownlie, McKillop, Main, Jenkins. Middle row: W. Struth (manager), McDonald, Hay, Simpson, Kennedy, Smith, Drysdale, McPhail, McHarg, Roberts, A. Dixon (trainer). Front row: Venters, Winning, Brown, McAuley, Meikeljohn, Kinnear, Gillick, Fiddes, Gray.

Rangers 1936-37. Back row, left to right: Dawson, Smith, Wallace, Simpson, Drysdale, Cheyne, Campbell, Thornton, Jenkins. Middle row: W. Struth (manager), Stewart, McPhail, Galloway, Soutar, McKillop, Reid, McKenzie, Fiddes, Turnbull, McDonald, A. Dixon (trainer). Front row: Kennedy, Gray, McLatchie, Venters, Hart, Meiklejohn, Main, Brown, Kinnear, Winning, MacAuley.

'Torry' Gillick joined Rangers from Petershill in 1933 and transferred to Everton for £8,000 in December 1935. A second spell with the club came after the war and Torry ended his career with Partick Thistle in 1951-52.

Outside right Jimmy Fiddes joined Rangers from Grange Rovers in season 1934-35 and was in and out of the side right up to the beginning of the Second World War in 1939. He starred for Falkirk and Stenhousemuir after the conflict.

Jimmy Simpson cost Rangers £1,000 from Dundee United in May 1927. A strong well-built centre-half, he went on to win numerous honours in the 1930s, including fourteen Scotland caps. His son Ronnie kept goal for Celtic and Scotland in the 1960s.

October 1945, and Rangers are about to depart for Germany, where they lost 6-1 to a British Combined Services side. Left to right: W. Struth (manager), Venters, Waddell, G. Brown (director), A. Dixon (trainer), David Gray, McColl, Dougie Gray, Dawson, A. L. Morton (director), Symon, Shaw, Woodburn, Johnstone, Duncanson, Williamson.

Rangers 1946-47. Back row, left to right: Sammy Cox, David Gray, George Young, Scot Symon, Jock Shaw. Front row: Willie Waddell, Torry Gillick, Willie Thornton, Jimmy Duncanson, Jimmy Caskie.

Rangers 1947-48. Back row, left to right: W. Struth (manager), Cox, Young, McColl, Brown, Woodburn, Watkins, Rae, R. McDonald (trainer). Front row: Waddell, Gillick, Shaw, Williamson, Thornton, Duncanson. Insets: Caskie and Rutherford.

The Rangers players about to board a plane for Lisbon in February 1948.

Rangers 1948-49. Back row, left to right: W. Struth (manager), Waddell, McColl, Young, Brown, Woodburn, Findlay, Rae, Duncanson, J. Smith (trainer). Front row: Rutherford, Gillick, Thornton, Shaw, Williamson, Cox, Caskie.

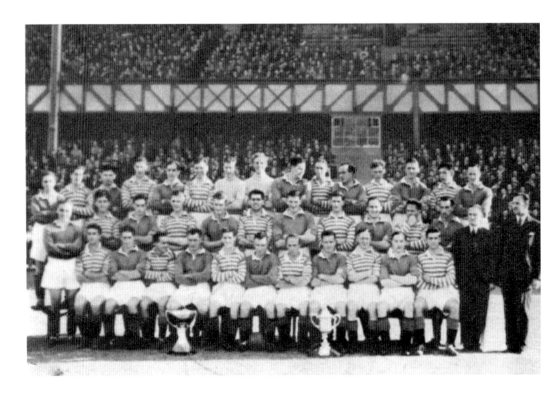

Rangers 1949-50. Back row, left to right: First team players only - Caskie, Marshall, Lindsay, Brown, Waddell, Little, Rutherford, Paton. Middle row: Williamson, McColl, Woodburn, Young, Rae, Findlay, J. Craven (asst. trainer), J. Smith (trainer). Front row: Cox, Gillick, Shaw, Thornton, Duncanson.

Rangers 1950-51. Back row, left to right: Willie Waddell, Ian McColl, George Young, Bobby Brown, Willie Woodburn, Sammy Cox. Front row: Billy Williamson, Willie Thornton, Jock Shaw, Jimmy Duncanson, Eddie Rutherford.

Rangers 1951-52. Back row, left to right: McColl, W. Boyd, J. Little, A. Elliott, R. Brown, G. Niven, J. Johnson, W. Rae, J. Forbes, E. Rutherford, A. Miller. Middle row: J. Smith (trainer), L. Blyth, W. Woodburn, A. McPhail, W. Waddell, W. McCulloch, W. Paton, W. Findlay, D. Stanners, R. Dunlop, J. Prentice, J. Pryde, W. Thornton, J. Craven (assistant trainer). Front row: Mr Struth (director-manager), W. Beckett, J. Hubbard, W. Simpson, S. Cox, R. Simpson, G. Young, D. Marshall, J. Woods, G. Scobie, J. Shaw, A. Simpson, W. Williamson.

SAMMY COX (Glasgow Rangers and Scotland) is a full-back who is one of the most difficult men for any opposing forward to elude. Playing for Scotland in partnership with George Young he has been the means of spoiling many a promising opening.

Sammy Cox played in the left back and left half positions for both Rangers and Scotland in the immediate post-war era. After three seasons with East Fife he emigrated to Canada in 1959.

Winger Willie Waddell was a star performer for both Rangers and Scotland. As a manager he won both the League Championship with Kilmarnock in 1965 and brought the European Cup Winners Cup to Ibrox in 1972.

Above left: Rangers director Alan Morton during his days as a player with the club in the 1920s. Morton got the nickname 'The Wee Society Man' due to his white-collar job as a mining engineer.

Above right: Left back and captain Jack Shaw got the nickname 'Tiger' because of his biting tackles. Born at Annathill in 1912, he cost Rangers £2,000 from Airdrieonians in the summer of 1938.

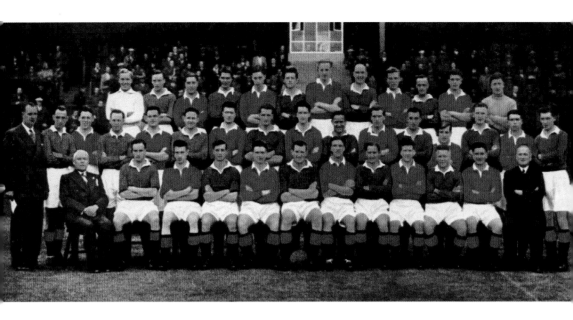

Rangers 1952-53. Back row, left to right: R. Brown, P. H. McMillan, A. Miller, J. Pryde, W. Boyd, W. Beckett, W. Gardiner, W. Rae, J. Forbes, J. Hubbard, E. Caldow, G. Niven. Middle row: J. Smith (trainer), W. Findlay, A. McPhail, W. Paton, W. McCulloch, W. Waddell, D. Stanners, W. Woodburn, W. R. Dunlop, W. Thornton, J. Prentice, A. Aikman, R. Simpson, G. McKenzie, I. Neillands, C. Liddell. Front row: Mr. W. Struth (director-manager), I. McColl, A. Elliott, R. J. Little, D. Marshall, G. Young (captain), W. Simpson, S. Cox, J. Woods, J. Shaw, G. Scobbie, J. Craven (assistant trainer).

Manager Bill Struth stands beside his portrait. The painting was presented to him at Glasgow's City Chambers in 1953.

Rangers 1953-54. Back row: Miller, Brown, Dunlop, Woodburn, McKenzie, Gardiner, Liddell, Little, Findlay, Niven, Hubbard. Middle row: Simpson, Niellands, Waddell, Paton, McColl, Stanners, Prentice, McCulloch, Boyd, Pryde, Elliott, Joe Craven (assistant trainer). Front row: William Struth (director-manager), P. H. McMillam, Shaw, H. McMillan, Cox, McIntosh, Young (capt), Caldow, Thornton, Brand, Grierson, Woods, Jimmy Smith. The two trophies shown are the Scottish Cup (right) and League Championship Cup.

Goalkeeper George Niven joined Rangers from Coupar Angus Juniors in December 1947. Originally understudy to Bobby Brown, he became a first team regular in 1952, and moved to Partick Thistle in 1962.

Rangers 1954-55.

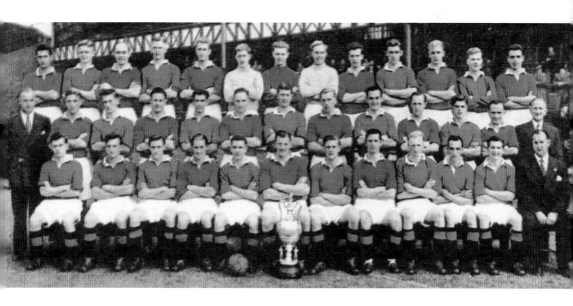

Rangers 1954-55. Back row: A. Simpson, G. Rogers, W. Rae, G. Mackenzie, W. Woodburn, G. Niven, J. Neill, R. Brown, R. Carmichael, C. Liddell, R. Menzies, J. Woods, I. Neillands. Centre row: S. Symon (manager), W. Simpson, A. Elliot, W. Waddell, J. Pryde, I. McColl, D. Stanners, J. Prentice, W. McCulloch, W. Paton, E. Caldow, J. Hubbard, J. Craven (assistant trainer). Front row: Hamish McMillian, D. Grierson, Hunter McMillan, S. Cox, D. McIntosh, G. Young, G. McKenzie, J. Little, W. Gardiner, W. Findlay, R. Brand, J. Smith (trainer).

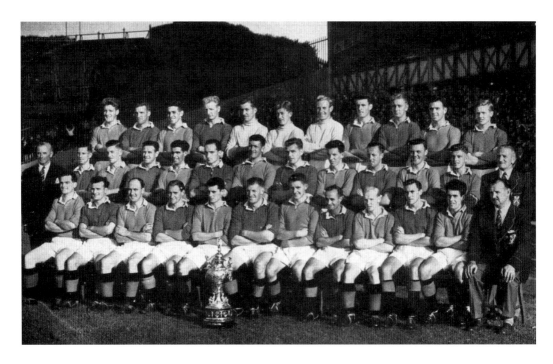

Glasgow Rangers, League Champions 1955-56.

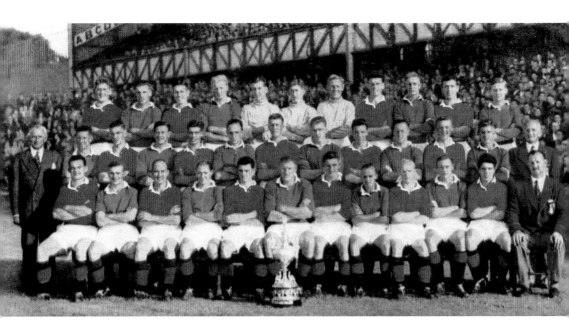

A colour photograph of the same 1955-56 team group taken from a different angle. Back row: Walker, Simpson, Boyd, Gardiner, Ritchie, Niven, Brow, Lawrie, Menzies, Neillands, Woods. Centre row: Scot Symon (manager), Little, Elliot, Waddell, Pryde, McColl, Stanners, Prentice, Murray, Paton, Thomson, Caldow, J. Craven (assistant trainer). Front row: McCulloch, Grierson, Rae, Cox, Queen, Young, Smith, Hubbard, Cunning, McMillan, Scott, Jimmy Smith (trainer).

South African Johnny Hubbard arrived at Ibrox in 1949. A clever wee outside left, he was also the club's penalty kick king, and scored a memorable second-half hat-trick against Celtic on New Year's Day 1955. He was sold to Bury for £6,000 in 1959.

Composed full back Eric Caldow signed professional forms for Rangers in 1952. A crisp tackler and a purveyor of the long probing pass he collected forty Scotland caps and represented the Scottish League on a further fourteen occasions. He moved to Stirling Albion in 1966.

Rangers 1956-57. Back row, left to right: Shearer, Caldow, Niven, McColl, Davis. Front row: Scott, Morrison, Murray, Young, Baird, Hubbard.

Rangers 1956-57. Back row, left to right: Paton, Menzies, Murray, Arniston, Niven, Ritchie, Logie, Simpson, Austin, Little. Middle row: S. Symon (manager), McColl, McCulloch, Baird, Moles, Kichenbrand, Walker, Prentice, Atkinson, Rae, McCorquodale, J. Craven (asst. trainer). Front row: Thomson, Caldow, Elliott, Grierson, Young, Smith, Shearer, Wilson, Hubbard, Dodds, D. Kinnear (trainer).

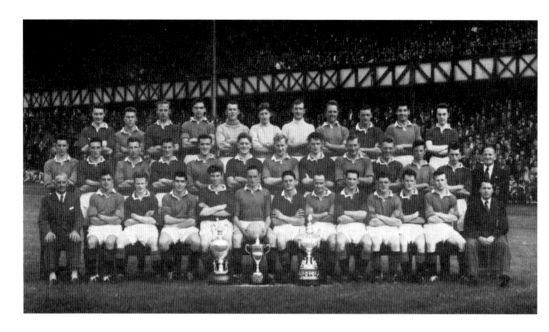

Rangers 1957-58. Back row, left to right: Smith, Millar, Atkinson, Logie, Wright, Niven, Ritchie, Valentine, Neil, Davis, Austin. Middle row: Murray, Currie, Simpson, Stevenson, Morrison, Walker, Baird, Moles, Kichenbrand, Thomson, Little, Queen, J. Craven (asst. trainer). Front row: S. Symon (manager), Caldow, Duncan, Scott, Robertson, McColl, McCorquodale, Hubbard, Brand, Shearer, Melrose, Wilson, D. Kinnear (trainer).

Born at Cumnock, Ayrshire on 14 May 1934, left back Eric Caldow arrived at Ibrox from Muirkirk Juniors in May 1952. A badly broken leg while playing for Scotland v. England at Wembley in 1963 ended his international career and saw Davie Provan take over the No. 3 jersey for Rangers on a regular basis.

Ian McColl was Rangers regular right half from 1945 to 1960. Appointed Scotland manager while still a player at Ibrox in November 1960, he became boss of Sunderland in 1965. Born at Alexandria on 7 June 1927, his grandfather, William McColl, starred for Renton and Scotland in the 1890s.

Rangers 1958-59. Back row, left to right: B. McIlroy, R. Brand, R. Orr, J. Currie, G. Niven, J. Little, N. Martin, W. Moles, A. Austin, D. Wilson, S. Mccorquodale. Centre row: J. Scot Symon (manager), J. Millar, W. Smith, W. Simpson, J. Valentine, S. Baird, W. Paterson, W. Telfer, H. Davis, W. Hogg, H. Neill, M. Murray, J. Craven (asst. trainer). Front row: G. Duncan, A. Scott, J. Queen, R. Shearer, A. McEwan, I. McColl, W. Stevenson, E. Caldow, A. Matthew, J. Hubbard, J. Provan, D. Kinnear (trainer).

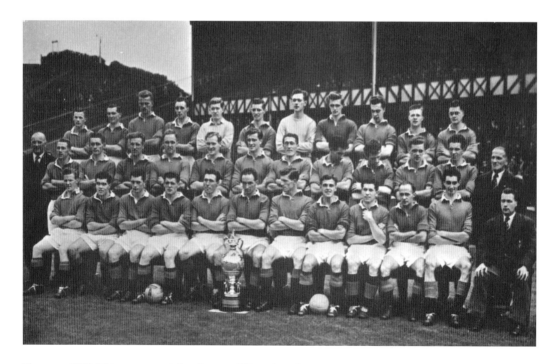

The same 1958-59 team group taken from a different angle.

Rangers 1959.

Above left: Right back Bobby Shearer cost Rangers £2,000 from Hamilton Academicals in December 1955. As a valued skipper and an uncompromising opponent he received the appropriate nickname of 'Captain Cutless'.

Above right: Jimmy Millar was a key forward for Rangers in the early 1960s. He arrived at Ibrox from Dumfermline Athletic in January 1955 and transferred to Dundee United during the summer of 1967.

Rangers 1960-61. Top, left to right: Bobby Shearer, Billy Ritchie, George Niven, Eric Caldow. Centre: Harold Davis, Bill Patterson, Jim Baxter. Bottom: Alec Scott, Ian McMillan, Jimmy Miller, Ralph Brand, Davie Wilson.

Above left: 'Slim Jim' Baxter cost Rangers £17,500 from Raith Rovers in June 1960. A skilful left half his passing and artistic flair in midfield was unsurpassed. Unfortunately a taste for the high life led to a premature end to his career in 1970.

Above right: 'Wee Willie' Henderson, Rangers wing wizard of the 1960s. Capped twenty-nine times by Scotland, he moved to Sheffield Wednesday in 1972 and spent a few years with Hong Kong Rangers before retiring.

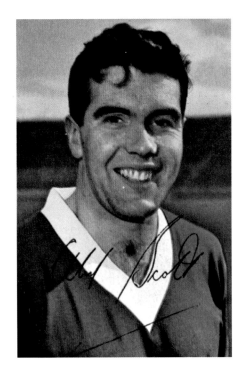 

Above left: Outside right Alex Scott was an explosive forward who usually sped down the wing and cut in field to deliver a powerful shot at goal. He was sold to Everton for £39,000 in February 1963.

Above right: Midfield maestro Ian McMillan cost the 'Light Blues' £10,000 from Airdrieonians in October 1958, and rejoined 'The Diamonds' six years later for half that amount.

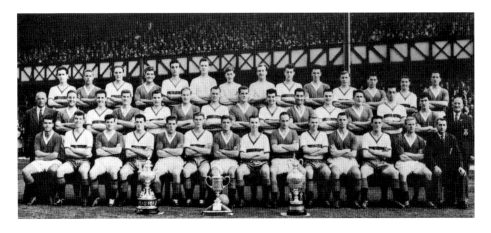

Rangers 1960-61. Back row, left to right: S. Anderson, J. Millar, J. Currie, B. Hume, R. McKinnon, G. Niven, W. Ritchie, B. Grant, M. Murray, W. Penman, A. Matthew, W. Henderson, R. Brand. Middle row: Scot Syman (manager), A. Franks, R. Evans, B. Stevenson, D. More, S. Baird, G. McLean, B. Paterson, B. King, H. Davis, R. Hynd, W. Telfer, D. Provan, J. Baxter, J. Craven. Front row: A. Scott, W. Cassidy, I. McMillan, J. Queen, B. Shearer, B. Young, E. Caldow, D. Bowie, I. McColl, C. Brown, J. Little, C. Watson, D. Wilson, D. Kinnear (trainer).

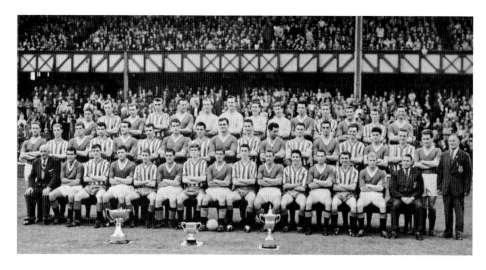

Rangers 1961-62. Back row, left to right: Henderson, Wood, Penman, Neil, McLean, Ritchie, Martin, McFarlane, Niven, Murray, Hunter, Hume, Burnside, Little. Middle row: Franks, Binnie, Stevenson, King, Mckinnon, More, Paterson, Evans, Baillie, Sutherland, Davis, Hynd, Provan, Greenwood, Baxter, Reid, Anderson, Craven (asst trainer). Front row: Scot Syman (manager), Scott, Watson, Christie, Willoughby, Shearer, Monney, Caldow, Greig, Millar, Forrest, Brand, S. Wilson, D. Wilson, Kinnear (trainer).

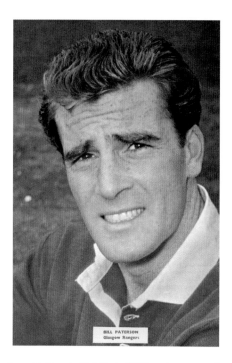

Above left: Goalkeeper Billy Ritchie arrived at Ibrox from Bathgate Thistle in 1955 and gave good service until joining Partick Thistle in 1968.

Above right: Centre half Bill Paterson cost Rangers a mere £3,500 from Newcastle United in July 1958, and made over one hundred appearances for the club before moving to Morton in 1962.

WILLIE HENDERSON
Rangers and Scotland

Outside right Willie Henderson replaced Alex Scott at Ibrox in the early 1960s. He ended his career at Airdrie and subsequently became a bookie and ran a pub in Belfast.

'Bleached blond' Davie Wilson joined Rangers from Baillieston Juniors in 1956. A goalscoring outside-left and a key member of both Rangers and Scotland's successful sides of the early 1960s.

Rangers 1962-63. Back row, left to right: Henderson, Marshall, Christie, Wood, Greig, Ritchie, McFarlane, Martin, Murray, R. Watson, Penman, Traill, Hume, Middle row: Binnie, King, Hunter, McKinnon, Evens, Paterson, Sutherland, Baillie, Hynd, Davis, Neil, Provan, Pickering, Baxter, J. Craven (asst. trainer). Front row: S. Symon (manager), Scott, Setterington, McMillan, Willoughby, Caldow, Mooney, Shearer, C. Watson, Millar, Forrest, Brand, Burnside, Wilson, D. Kinnera (trainer).

Photograph of the same 1962-63 team group taken from a different angle.

Rangers 1963. Back row, left to right: Bobby Shearer, Eric Caldow, Harold Davis, Davie Provan, Billy Ritchie, Ronnie McKinnon, John Greig, Jim Baxter. Front row: S. Symon (manager), Willie Henderson, George McLean, Ian McMillan, Jimmy Millar, Ralph Brand, Davie Wilson, D. Kinnear (trainer).

Scottish Cup Winners 1963.

The ball is in the safe hands of Billy Ritchie, Rangers regular between the posts in the sixties. 'The Quiet Man' ended his playing career with Motherwell in 1972.

Above left: Hard as nails full back Bobby Shearer moved to Queen of the South in 1965. Capped four times by Scotland, he was manager of Third Lanark when the Cathkin club folded in 1967.

Above right: Davie Wilson had a great 1962 for club and country. He scored six in a 7-1 victory over Falkirk on 17 March, netted for Scotland in a 2-0 win against England on 14 April, and returned to Hampden the following week to convert again as Rangers defeated St Mirren 2-0 in the Scottish Cup Final.

Rangers 1963-64. Back row, left to right: Shearer, caldow, Provan, Ritchie, Greig, McKinnon, Baxter. Front row: S. Symon (manager), Henderson, McMillan, McLean, Millar, Forrest, Brand, Wilson, D. Kinnear (trainer).

A black and white photograph of the same 1963-64 team group taken from a different angle.

Rangers 1963-64. Back row, left to right: Shearer, Provan, Ritchie, Greig, McKinnon, Baxter. Front row: Henderson, Millar, Forrest, Brand, C. Watson.

Rangers play the blues: Jim Forrest, Bobby Shearer, Craig Watson, Alex Willoughby, Ronnie McKinnon and Billy Ritchie.

JOHN GREIG
Rangers

Half back John Greig signed for Rangers from Whitburn in 1960, and provided the side with many inspirational performances over the next two decades.

Rangers 1963-64. Back row, left to right: Wood, Forrest, Christie, C. Watson, Ritchie, McFarlane, Martin, Hunter, Mathieson, McKinnon, McLardy, Willoughby. Middle row: Marshall, Greig, Neil, Davis, Sutherland, Baillie, Hynd, Provan, Jackson, McLean, R. Watson, Baxter, Pickering, J. Craven (asst. trainer). Front row: S. Symon (manager), Henderson, McCartney, McMillan, Setterington, Caldow, Mooney, Shearer, Thomson, Millar, Burnside, Brand, Traill, Wilson, D. Kinnear (trainer).

Rangers 1964-65. Back row, left to right: Wood, Mathieson, C. Watson, Stewart, B. Watson, Rennie, Martin, W. Ritchie, McFarlane, Donnelly, Forrest, Mooney, Willoughby, Reid, Traill. Centre: McCartney, Greig, Mair, McKinnon, Jackson, Hynd, Simpson, Baillie, D. Ritchie, Provan, Sutherland, McLean, King, Baxter, McLardie, Joe Craven (asst. trainer). Front: Scot Symon (manager), Henderson, Johnston, McMillan, Setterington, Caldow, Smith, Shearer, Thomson, Millar, Semple, Brand, Vint, Wilson, David Kinnear (trainer). Trophies won last season are in the foreground (left to right): Scottish Cup, Second XI Cup, League Championship Trophy and Scottish League Cup.

Rangers 1965-66. Left to right: Provan, Greig, McKinnon, G. McLean, Watson, Ritchie, Johansen, Millar, Johnston, Forrest, Sorensen, Willoughby, Wilson, Henderson.

Rangers 1965-66. Back row, left to right: Willoughby, Stewart, C. Watson, Paterson, R. Watson, McGillivray, W. Ritchie, Martin, McFarlane, McLardy, Beck, W. Jardine, Mathieson, W. Smith, Traill. Middle row: Johansen, Donnelly, Greig, Jackson, McKinnon, D. Ritchie, Provan, Simpson, Hynd, Sutherland, McLean, McCartney, Wood, J. Craven (asst. trainer). Front row: S. Symon (manager), Henderson, Paul, Millar, Reid, Forrest, Setterington, Caldow, Semple, Brand, J. Jardine, Johnston, Vint, Wilson, D. Kinnear (trainer).

Rangers 1966-67. Back row, left to right: Jardine, Johansen, Martin, Provan, McKinnon, Greig. Front row: Henderson, A. Smith, Hynd, D. Smith, Johnston.

Centre half Ronnie McKinnon signed for Rangers in July 1959 from Dunipace Juniors. Capped twenty-eight times by Scotland, his twin brother Donnie, played for Partick Thistle in the 1960s.

Rangers 1966-67.

Rangers 1967-68. Back row, left to right: S. Symon (manager), R. Watson, Provan, McKinnon, Sorenson, Martin, Ritchie, Hynd, Jardine, Persson, Seith (asst. trainer). Front row: D. White (asst. manager), Henderson, A. Smith, Willoughby, Ferguson, Greig, D. Smith, Penman, Johansen, Johnston, D. Kinnear (trainer).

John Greig, 'The Greatest Rangers Player' in action against Dundee United at Tannadice in the 1969-70 season.

Manager Scott Symon in conversation with his assistant Davie White at Ibrox. Within a few months, Symon was sacked and White took over as boss.

Rangers 1967-68.

A colour photograph of the same team group taken from a different angle.

Rangers 1968-69. Back row, left to right: Alex, Smith, White, Jackson, Stirling, Sorensen, Martin, McDermott, Keddie, Persson, Conn, Mathieson. Middle: Lawrie Smith (physio.). Bobby Watson, Kenny Watson, Provan, Wood, McKinnon, Jimmy Johnstone, Hynd, Miller, Davie Smith, Cairns, Johansen, Evans, Jardine. Front: Davie Kinnear (trainer), Henderson, Laing, Willoughby, Setterington, Ferguson, Davie White (manager), Greig, McPhee, Penman, Herron, Semple, Joe Craven (asst. trainer). Notable absentee from the group is Willie Johnston, who had a septic foot.

Rangers 1969-70.

Rangers 1970-71. Back row, left to right: Conn, Stein, Donaldson, Neef, McCloy, Jackson, R. Watson, D. Stevenson, N. Stevenson, Fyfe, I. MacDonald. Middle row: J. Wallace (coach), T. Craig (physio), K. Watson, Mathieson, Renton, McKinnon, Miller, Jardine, Johnstone, D. Smith, McCallum, J. Craven (asst. trainer), S. Anderson (trainer), Front row: W. Waddell (manager), Henderson. Semple, A. MacDonald, Alexander, Greig, Parlane, Penman, Morrison, Johnston, W. Thornton (asst. manager).

Rangers 1971-72.

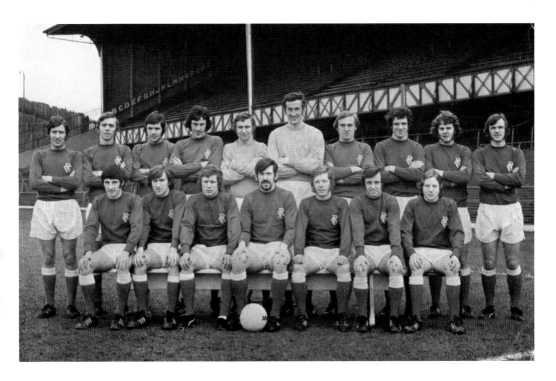

Rangers 1972, Barcelona bound. Back row, left to right: Jardine, Miller, Johnstone, Jackson, Neef, McCloy, Stein, D. Smith, Conn, Mathieson. Front row: Denny, Fyfe, Johnston, Greig, A. MacDonald, McLean, I. MacDonald.

Rangers 1972-73.

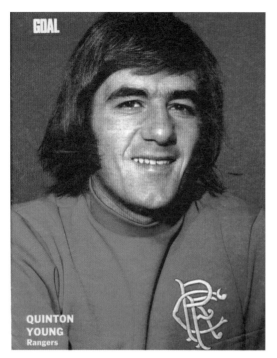

Outside left Quinton Young.

Centre forward Derek Parlane.

Inside left Alex MacDonald.

Left half Dave Smith.

Rangers 1973. Back row: A. Miller, T. Forsyth, D. Johnstone, D. Parlane, P. McCloy, G. Neef, D. Smith, J. Denny, B. Mathieson. Front row: A. Conn, S. Jardine, T. McLean, Q. Young, J. Greig, A. MacDonald, J. Mason, J. Wallace (manager).

Rangers 1973-74. Back row, left to right: Young, Struthers, Scott, Jackson, Hunter, McCloy, Kennedy, Forsyth, Burke, Donaldson, McNichol. Middle row: T. Craig (physio), I. MacDonald, Hamilton, O'Hara, Conn, D. Smith, Johnstone, Miller, Thomson, Mathieson, Fyfe, McDougall, S. Anderson (trainer). Front row: J. Wallace (manager), Morris, McLean, A. MacDonald, Houston, Parlane, Greig, Jardine, Mason, Steel, Q. Young, Denny, W. Thornton (asst. manager).

Rangers 1975-76. Back row, left to right: Miller, Forsyth, Parlane, Stein, Kennedy, Johnstone, Jackson, Scott, O'Hara. Front row: McLean, McDougall, McKean, MacDonald, Jardine, Greig, Hamilton, Young, Fyfe, Denny.

Rangers 1976-77. Back row, left to right: Miller, Parlane, Henderson, Kennedy, McCloy, Lawrie, Jackson, Watson, Forsyth. Middle row: T. Craig (physio), McDougall, Brand, Robertson, Stein, Johnstone, A. Boyd, Armour, O'Hara, Dawson, J. Mason (trainer). Front row: J. Wallace (manager), McLean, G. Boyd, Morris, Jardine, Greig, Denny, MacDonald, MacKean, Munro, Hamilton.

Tom Forsyth moved from Motherwell to Ibrox for £40,000 in October 1972. Originally an inside right he was converted into a more defensive midfield position at half back in 1974. Nicknamed 'Jaws' because of his biting tackles, this fearless competitor received twenty-two Scotland caps.

Rangers 1978-79. Back row, left to right: Miller, Parlane, Jackson, McCloy, Kennedy, Forsyth, Watson, A. Boyd. Middle row: T. Craig (physio), Morris, Richardson, Brand, Johnstone, Smith, Armour, Dawson, Denny, J. Mason (trainer). Front row: J. Greig (manager), Mackay, Roberston, McLean, Jardine, J. MacDonald, Cooper, A. MacDonald, Russell, Strickland.

Rangers 1979-80. Back row, left to right: A. Forsyth, Miller, Parlane, Richardson, Jackson, McCloy, Kennedy, McIntosh, T. Forsyth, Watson, McLaren. Middle row: Stan Anderson (coach), Robertson, Stirton, Dalziel, Smith, Armour, Dawson, Denny, Urquhart, Matthews, Morris. Front row" John Greig (manager), Mackay, McLean, Strickland, Jardine, Johnstone, Cooper, A. MacDonald, Russell, J. MacDonald, Tom Craig (physio), Joe Mason (coach).

Rangers 1980-81. Back row, left to right: Stirton, Stevens, Jackson, McAdam, Young, McCloy, Marshall, McIntosh, T. Forsyth, K. Watson, Clark. Middle row: D. Provan (scout), S. Anderson (trainer), G. Watson, Lyall, Miller, Richardson, Redford, Bett, Urquhart, Dalziel, Robertson, A. Forsyth, T. Craig (physio). Front row: J. Greig (manager), Davies, McLean, J. MacDonald, Jardine, Johnstone, Cooper, Russell, A. MacDonald, MacKay, J. Mason (trainer).

Soccer Sixes Winners 1983-84. Back row, left to right: Bruce, Redford, Nicholl, Mitchell, Dawson, A. Totten (coach). Front row: Davies, McClelland, D. Ferguson, Williamson, Cooper.

Rangers 1983-84. Back row, left to right: MacKinnon, Dawson, McCoist, Prytz. Middle row: Redford, Stevens, Paterson, McCloy, McPherson, Clark, Cooper. Front row: Lyall, MacDonald, McClelland, Davies, Russell.

Rangers 1983-84. Back row, left to right: Prytz, Russell, McAdam, Walker, McCloy, Nicholl, McCoist, Cooper. Middle row: J. Wallace (manager), S. Anderson (youths), Fraser, Clark, Paterson, McPherson, Mitchell, Redford, Burns, R. Findlay (physio). Front row: J. Hagart (reserves), MacDonald, Williamson, Dawson, McClelland, Mackay, Munro, A. Totten (coach).

Rangers 1984-85. Back row, left to right: Prytz, D. Ferguson, McFarlane, Kennedy, McPherson, McClelland, Paterson, McAdam, Mitchell, E. Ferguson, Munro, Fleck. Middle row: S. Anderson (youths), Lindsay, Davies, Durrant, S. Fraser, Walker, McCloy, Bruce, Burns, MacKinnon, Leeman, Connor, R. Findlay (physio). Front row: Redford, Dawson, I. Ferguson, Williamson, Cooper, A. Totten (coach), J. Wallace (manager), J. Hagart (reserves), Clark, C. Fraser, McCoist, Russell, MacDonald.

Rangers 1984-85. Back row, left to right: Prytz, Russell, Burns, Clark, Williamson, McCoist, Munro. Middle row: A. Totten (coach), R. Findlay (physio), McAdam, McPherson, Walker, McClelland, McCloy, Paterson, Mitchell, S. Anderson (youths), J. Hagart (reserves). Front row: Redford, Dawson, Cooper, Fraser, J. Wallace (manager), E. Ferguson, MacKinnon, MacDonald, I. Ferguson.

Rangers 1985-86. Back row, left to right: MacKinnon, Munro, McFarlane, Nisbet, McPherson, Paterson, E. Ferguson, Beattie, Dawson, D. Ferguson. Middle row: Prytz, Durrant, Fraser, McMinn, Bruce, McCloy, Walker, Johnstone, Burns, Davies, Miller. Front row: S. Anderson (youths), MacDonald, I. Ferguson, Williamson, Cooper, A. Totten (coach), J. Wallace (manager), J. Hagart (reserves), Russell, McCoist, Redford, Fleck, R. Findlay (physio).

Rangers 1986-87. Back row, left to right: McCoist, Nicholl, Burns, Walker, Nisbet, McPherson, Woods, West, McMinn, Cooper, W. Smith (asst. manager). Front row: Munro, Fraser, Dawson, Souness (player/manager), Butcher, Durrant, D. Ferguson, Russell, Fleck.

Rangers 1987-88. Back row, left to right: Francis, Munro, McCoist, Cohen, Nicholl, Roberts, Cooper. Middle row: P. Boersma (coach), MacGregor, Gough, Walker, Woods, Falco, Phillips, W. Smith (asst. manager). Front row: Durrant, D. Ferguson, Souness (player/manager), Butcher, McCall, Fleck.

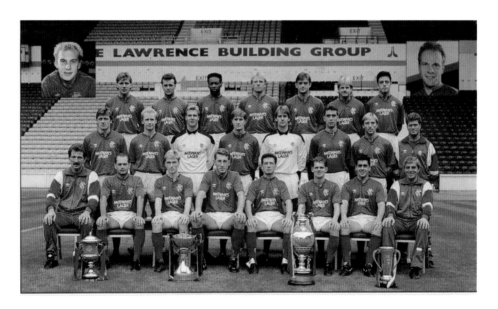

Rangers 1988-89. Back row, left to right: McCoist, Cooper, Walters, MacGregor, Drinkell, Munro, Kirkwood. Middle row: Phillips, Brown, Woods, Gough, Walker, Nisbet, Stevens, P. Boersma (coach). Front row: Souness (player/manager), Wilkins, T. Ferguson, Gough, D. Ferguson, Durrant, McCall, W. Smith (manager).

Rangers 1991-92.

Scottish Champions 1992. Back row, left to right: Huistra, Spackman, D. Robertson, Hateley, McCall, Durrant, Goram. Front row: McCoist, L. Roberston, Gordon, Gough, A. Roberston, Nisbet, Rideout, Kuznetsov.

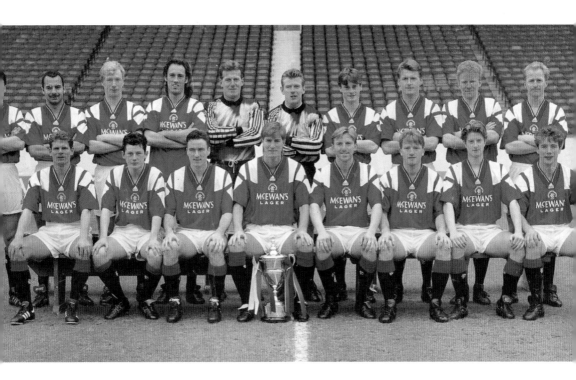

May 1992. The Rangers team photographed in their new strip with the recently won League Championship trophy.

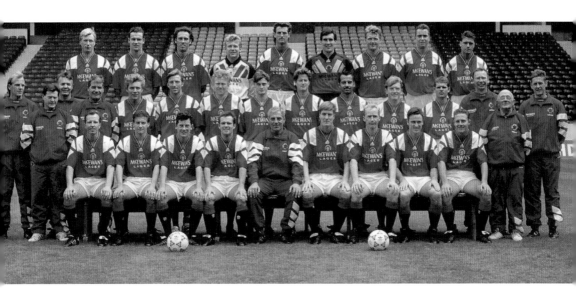

Rangers 1992-93. Back row, left to right: Mikhailitchenko, Reid, Hateley, Goram, McPherson, Maxwell, Spackman, Nisbet, Rideout. Middle row: J. McGregor (reserves), J. Bell (kit), W. Collins (physio), A. Knox (asst. manager), McCoist, Stevens, Kuznetsov, D. Robertson, Gordon, McCall, Durrant, D. Dodds (coach), G. Soutar (asst. kit), W. Kirkwood (coach). Front row: Steven, Vinnicombe, A. Robertson, Spencer, W. Smith (manager), Gough, Brown, Ferguson, McSwegan.

Goalkeeper Andy Goram cost Rangers £1 million from Hibernian in the summer of 1991, and gave the Ibrox club brilliant service over the next seven seasons. Capped forty-three times by Scotland, on leaving the 'Light Blues' in 1998, Andy had outings for a good number of clubs, including Motherwell, Manchester United, Coventry City and Queen of the South before retiring midway through season 2003-04.

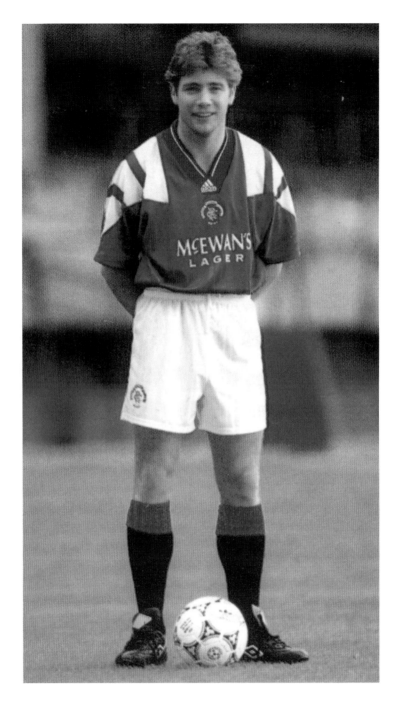

Goalscorer Ally McCoist began his professional career at St Johnstone in 1978, and signed for Sunderland for either £350,000 or £400,000 depending on which report you believe, in August 1981. His two seasons on Wearside were none too productive and he returned north to join Rangers at a cut-price of £185,000 in 1983. For the next fifteen years 'Super Ally' hit the back of the net with monotonous regularity - 355 goals in 581 competitive appearances (and that total doesn't include his hat trick against Celtic in the Glasgow Cup Final at Ibrox in 1986). Capped sixty-one times by Scotland, he became Rangers manager in 2011.

The 1996-97 Rangers squad which captured the ninth league title in a row.

Above left: Skilful inside forward Paul Gascoigne was a law unto himself both on and off the football field. He starred for Newcastle United and Spurs before joining Rangers from Lazio for £4.3 million in the summer of 1995.

Above right: Like 'Gazza', Danoish Internationalist Brian Laudrup was a dribbling genius. His clubs include Bronby, Bayer Uerlingen and Bayern Munich, and he joined Rangers from Fiorentina, after a period on loan to AC Milan, in July 1994. A European Championship winner in 1992, his brother Michael is the current boss at Swansea.

The Rangers players celebrate taking the first SPL title in 1999.

Rangers 1999-2000. Back row, left to right: Feeney, Johansson, Vidmar, Niemi, Klos, Brown, Albertz, Wilson, Moore, Hendry. Middle row: Van Lingen (asst. manager), Nicholson, B. Ferguson, Kanchelskis, Negri, Adamczuk. Front row: Wallace, McCann, van Bronkhorst, Amoruso, D. Advocaat (manager), Numan, Mols, Reyna.

Captain Barry Ferguson holds up the SPL trophy after Rangers 6-1 victory over Dumfermline at Ibrox, a result which secured the 2002-03 Championship title.

Rangers celebrate their 2003 Scottish Cup Final win over Dundee thanks to an Amoruso headed goal.

Rangers 2003-04, photographed with the spoils of the previous treble winning season.

Rangers 2011-12. A season which proved to be one of the most traumatic in the club's long and illustrious history.

Manager Ally McCoist—hoping to take Rangers back into SFPL Premiership in the near future.